The ABC's of GRATITUDE

How to be GRATEFUL when things are not so GREAT

L.S. Maiten

Copyright 2019 by L.S. Maiten, LLC.

L.S.Maiten, LLC.

Jacksonville, FL. 32204

www.lsmaiten.com

All rights reserved. No portion of this book may be reproduced, stored in a retrieval system, or transmitted in any form or by any means-electronic, mechanical, photocopy, recording, or otherwise- except for brief quotations-without prior written permission of the publisher.

Unless otherwise noted scripture quotations are taken from the New King James Version. Copyright 1982 by Thomas Nelson. Used by permission.

Scripture quotations marked KJV are from the King James Version. Public Domain.

L.S. Maiten

The ABC's of Gratitude: How to be GRATEFUL when things are not so GREAT

Published by: L.S. Maiten, LLC

Cover & Graphic Designs by: Dominique Pugh

Edited by: Jerra Latrice

Photographer: Tori Watts

ISBN: 978-0-578-22807-5

10 9 8 7 6 5 4 3 2 1

To order wholesale copies of book please contact 904-405-0378.

Printed in the United States of America.

I dedicate this piece of art to my beloved daughter,

Kayla A. Maiten

v

Content

Introduction...1

Part 1: Self Awareness................................4

A Attitude vs Adjustments......................................5

B Boundaries vs Bruises..7

C Conflict vs Commitment.....................................10

D Disappointments vs Deliverance...........................12

E Entitlement vs Experience...................................14

F Forgiveness vs Future..16

G GED vs GYM..18

H Habits vs Health...20

Part 2: Job/Career/Business........................22

I Incarceration vs Information................................23

J Job vs Joy..25

K Knight vs Knowledge...27

L Long-suffering vs Longevity................................29

M Mistakes vs Ministry..31

N Not yet vs Now..33

O Oppression vs Opportunity..................................35

Part 3: Relationships 37

P Processing Parenting......................................38
Q Quality vs Quantity..40
R Rejection vs Reflection..................................42
S Separation vs Strength...................................44
T Traditions vs Teachings................................47

Part 4: Faith...50

U Understanding Upgrades..............................51
V Victim vs Vision..53
W Want vs Wisdom...55
X X-ray your heart 57
Y Young vs Youthfulness................................59
Z Zealous Servant...61

Epilogue..63
References...65
Meet the Author...66

Introduction

Everyone has experienced those not so great days, weeks, months and maybe even years. I decided to write this book when things in my life were not so great, and I was ungrateful for my own life. I would also be around others who wasn't so grateful for their life either, so that didn't help my negative mindset at the time. How did I get here you may ask? At the time I thought it was just one thing, but honestly it was several things that build up over years to this point. Unfortunately, I had to leave the place where I laid my head to rest, shut down my growing local business that I invested in for three years, despised my off and on legal career, lost a close friend and business partner just to name a few. I realized in those three to four years, I sacrificed so much - my family, time, finances, health and most importantly, my faith. And to be completely honest, it was because of my own disobedience. Needless to say, I failed flat on my face. Starting over once again, meaning- I've been down this road before, it didn't look so hopeful for me. This road may have not been the same exact route, but its "landscapes" surely looked familiar. It was terrifying knowing I had limited resources and a growing child to take care of who was counting on me. I felt like a complete failure. Question: Why do we sometimes put ourselves in chaotic situations, then feel pathetic about what we got ourselves into? Why the hell do we do this??

While contemplating my next move for my life, something hit me- I call it my spirit. Oftentimes, I repeat the phrase "I know where my help comes from". This is what my spirit, that still, soft voice was telling me during this plight. Even though I would encourage and recite the phrase to others, I wasn't applying that faith to my own circumstances. The disturbing thing is that I even started to think to myself I didn't deserve this, I should be doing this or have this by now, etc. That phrase kept replaying in my mind, and I wasn't trying to hear it. Nope! I had a real attitude. Although, I knew my life and current situation that I put myself in could have been much worse, I still had a distasteful disposition about what I was going through. Oh, but let me tell you I truly believe God, the universe, or whomever you choose to name it, has an interesting way of grabbing our attention! Things did get worse! It wasn't until I humbled myself and looked back on how God has taken care of me before, and how things could have really gone even more sour than I could imagine. One word resonated with me- grateful.

    Allow me to remind you, for three to four years or probably longer, I neglected my faith, so I definitely was not thinking of any kind of bible scriptures, motivational sermons, nor prayer. Nope, I didn't even pray. I completely turned my back on God, and truthfully, I did not know how to call on Him because I was too ashamed. This wasn't a relationship I could just pick up where we left off. Once again my spirit hit me, but this time it occurred when I saw my daughter crying at the end of the bed, because she saw me upset and worried. She said something that was so profound- "Ma, I can't wait till we make it". I guess I had an idea what she meant. I immediately knew I couldn't afford to quit life and wallow in my own self-pity. In that moment, I knew my circumstances were larger than myself. I started to pray by simply talking to God and asking for forgiveness, since I was not grateful for life itself. I couldn't just think about being grateful, I had to open my mouth and profess it! Sometimes when I didn't know what to say in my prayers, I'll just say *Lord, I thank you*. This is exactly what gratitude is...being thankful.

Yes, I still have to be intentional about being grateful. It gets better each and every day. Completely grateful for still having air to breathe and not needing a machine to do so, clothes to choose from and not having to receive hand-me-downs, grateful that I am in my right mind to complete daily tasks and be creative, and a beautiful daughter who is alive and well. Being grateful is a conscious decision. Even if this is not your testimony and you are on a breathing machine or you actually do have an unhealthy child, you too my friend still can be grateful. I believe once we realize how things could be severely worse in this thing called life (in the words of the late great musician Prince song) than what we're going through this is when you can learn to gain gratitude, as I did.

This devotional book is for those who still have to say their whole ABC's out loud when they stuck after J or Q. I'm kidding! But seriously, this is for us who have to be reminded to be grateful when things are not so great. I pray my testimonies and short stories of success and failures help you with your test. Be encouraged, my friend and please note that we all have a story.

"She opens her mouth with wisdom, and the teaching of kindness is on her tongue."

- Proverbs 31:26

Part 1: SELF-AWARENESS

TO KNOW THYSELF IS THE FOUNDATION OF EVERYTHING GREAT!

-L.S.Maiten

Attitude vs. Adjustments

"If you don't like something, change it. If you can't change it, change your attitude."

-Dr. Maya Angelou

How often growing up did your parents say "Change your attitude, or you need an attitude adjustment?" Guilty! I now have to say it to my teenage daughter every now-and-then. Children are not the only ones that have this attitude issue - adults have it too. Why do adults get these attitudes though? One answer- because things are not going the way we want them to. Just like children who aren't getting their way. Sorry to hurt your feelings, but this is childish!

Remember in the introduction I mentioned how I lost my place where I was staying, well this happened to me twice within two months. When I left the home I was sharing with my business partner, I went to live with my uncle and his fiancé. I looked forward to saving money and getting back on my feet. I had just lost my business, and oftentimes, that puts a dent in your assets. In other words, I went broke! Savings account vanished! No money! It took a lot for me to find the courage to ask my uncle to stay with him just for a few months. Of course I offered to pay something for my time there. Anyone who really knows me knew that had to be difficult for me to do - ask for help. I never liked being placed in positions where I needed someone to that extent.

For this reason: Well, you know how someone tries to tell you something without saying it, so they won't look or feel bad. Listen to this - I moved in with my uncle mid-November and was told without saying it clearly I would have to find somewhere else to go after all the holidays.

I had an attitude out of this world after that one-and-a- half-minute unclear, lukewarm, apathetic conversation with my uncle. I called my mom, sister, and a few friends to vent my frustrations to. I found myself wondering all kinds of things - like *what the hell*, first of all. How could he do this to me? I'm his niece! Doesn't he see I'm trying to take care of my daughter? Was it because my dog was there too? I asked him if could I bring it before I came. Or maybe it was because his fiancé wanted her space back in the guest room. My mind went everywhere. I guess I had no choice at this point, but to look for another place. I had to make a quick adjustment.

I moved out less than 30 days of being at my uncle's place. After much praying and searching for something suitable for my daughter and I to live, I found a perfect spacious two-bedroom apartment in central downtown. However, it wasn't until I humbled myself and became grateful that my uncle opened his home to us initially. Just think I'm grown and no one really owes me anything, yet I was still blessed to have somewhere to stay. How in the world could I have had an attitude? In those couple of weeks that I lived with my uncle, I actually learned a lot about myself- (1) I didn't like asking for help, because I didn't want to be

rejected, (2) I'm resilient. When it's time to bust an urgent move, I don't procrastinate, and (3) I always went to friends and family first to talk, and not God. It was clear, I still had some more adjustments to make. Consider this my friend, adjust your attitude about the adjustments you may have to make, and you will receive a blessing in the midst of your gratitude.

Boundaries vs. Bruises

"A person can do himself more harm than others can do him."

-Barbara Kipfer

When my late ex-husband and I were stationed in Georgia, we were only 19 and 20 years old. A lot of the military soldiers and their spouses were around the same age as well-very young. I was introduced to all types of cultures, people, and lifestyles. We lived in a two-story complex apartment, off the military base, with a sizable living and dining room connection, with light color carpet and a nice balcony off the living room area. We absolutely loved our first marital home together. Three months after being there, we gained new neighbors right downstairs from us. It was a peculiar looking couple, the husband was Jamaican and his wife was Pakistan with a handsome three-year-old boy.

Chris, my ex-husband became quite acquainted with the Jamaican husband very early on because they would carpool to work most of the time together. Although the wife and I were both stay-at-home moms, we didn't see each other often. I didn't think anything of not seeing her much until we heard a lot of screaming arguments downstairs. Growing up in a domestic violence environment, as I did, I was aware of certain noises. But it still wasn't clear what was going on until I asked Gary, the husband while sitting outside on our balcony with Chris having a drink, "Where was Carmen...?" I said "She's welcome to come over." He said, "No she won't be coming out." You know what I was thinking after that...*Hmmm I know what the hell is going on now*. I just said "Ok." Chris and I then looked at each other in a strange, but connected way. I could tell we both were thinking the same thing. Gary started to laugh and jokingly saying "She doesn't like hanging with me" and other little silly things. Maybe the alcohol was starting to tell who he really was. His comments were not sitting well with me, so I didn't see him for the rest of the day. Days, probably even weeks went by, and we didn't see either one of them.

  I would never forget one early morning at 2:00am, Carmen came banging on our door, saying "Help me, please let me in!" I didn't even think this woman could get that loud! Chris and I woke up startled, he ran to the door and I went to our newborn's room to look out the window and to assure that my baby didn't wake up. Carmen came in crying with her lip busted, face bruised, clothes ripped, and her three-year-old son in her arms crying as well. She had been abused by her husband. Of course, Gary came upstairs drunk looking for her and demanding her to leave with him, but she was so terrified she kept saying that she wanted to wait for the police to talk at all while shaking. Chris drew up a boundary immediately and did not let him in. Gary was in a rage. Later we found out that Gary was an alcoholic and have been abusing Carmen for the last three years of their 4-year marriage. Carmen was a woman who spoke little English and was isolated from her family, who lived overseas. Her culture taught her to never leave her husband and that she had no say so in her relationship, so she overlooked his behavior, and drew no boundaries for herself or their child.

  Moreover, her boundaries were often disrespected. Our boundaries are to keep us safe and stand firm on healthy values and decisions, not to isolate nor put us in harm's way. That early morning when the police showed up to gather Carmen's report, we helped her get some of her things off the floor that was covering some dark old blood stains on her light color carpet. She proceeds to say "I lost sight of who I once was and how a man should treat a woman, but I'm grateful that these people opened up their doors to me." Please note: You can't overcome anything you keep overlooking.

Conflict vs. Commitment

"Stay committed to your decisions, but stay flexible in your approach."

- Tony Robbins

In 2014, Lebron James made the decision to return back to his hometown Cleveland, Ohio to play basketball. I personally was disappointed, because being a Floridian, I liked him playing with the Miami Heat. I wouldn't say it was a huge conflict with Miami fans compared to Cleveland fans upon his departure from there in 2010, but it did stir up some controversy. When James made his decision to go to South Beach, there was a huge broadcast called Miami Heat Welcome Party, while on stage with Chris Bosh and the 3-time champion, finals MVP Dwyane Wade, he stated "Not two, not three, not four, not five, not six, not seven." Ok, when he got to saying not 5 and 6- I knew this wasn't going to end well. I said you doing too much! For those who have no idea what I'm talking about with these numbers...he was talking about winning championships with the Miami Heat. Well, in 2012, he made the decision to leave the owner of Miami Heat, Pat Riley, and the organization.

James, has always told Cleveland that would be his home and when he finally won a championship with the Cavaliers in 2016, he said "Cleveland this one is for you"! Cleveland Cavaliers accepted Lebron James back with open arms, because of his commitment to them. Let me ask you something: Are you so committed to something that you don't want to stir up any conflict, or is someone grateful to have you on their squad, because of your commitment? Oftentimes, what we value as a way of shifting our commitments and what we hold dear to us has a way of showing our gratitude. This is sometimes uncomfortable, but when you know who you are, you find a way to embrace the conflicts life sometimes brings even in those not so great times.

Disappointments vs. Deliverance

"Just because God is reliable does not mean he's predictable"

-Pastor Terry Anderson, Houston,TX.

    Disappointments are inevitable. They have a way of causing us to lose confidence, courage, and certainty. In 2015, I remember how excited I was to receive the news I was approved to buy a new home. With my prior credit history and inability to remain at a job long-term, I was surprised to get approved at such a good rate. Everything was in place for once, so I thought. Buying a new home was an unknown journey for me, somewhat terrifying. I thought of things like what if something breaks or needs to be replaced, it was all on me and not maintenance personnel in an apartment complex this time around. When purchasing anything big, one must do extensive homework. Sometimes this means if something drastic happens you have enough in savings to cover your mortgage. I did not.

    My realtor called me at work on a Friday afternoon right before I was ready to set off my weekend with either Prince or T.I. on my radio gladly, he said these exact words: "Ms. Maiten we are so sorry to inform you that the home you had your eyes on was mistakenly sold earlier today." I think I went silent at least 30 seconds. "How in the world does this happen?" I thought. How can someone buy my house from me just that quick!? I was so upset and started cussing and fussing. I wasn't so "Christian-like" in that moment. It was a disappointment to the highest degree. Not only did I find out the guy who bought the home had cash to buy it, but I also found out my paperwork was not even presented to the underwriters correctly.

God always seems to amaze me. He will protect us from danger and disappointments that could have destroyed us for years with mental torture. Two months later after that awful news from the realtor, my job closed down. Getting that home at the time would have been financial suicide for me. Stressful bigtime! It was then that I knew I had been delivered from a future disaster. I encourage you to be grateful for disappointments, because that's where you may meet your deliverance. Rather you find yourself not getting accepted into school that you dreamed of or a heartbreaking experience of any kind- you too can find gratitude in it. Everything happens for a reason.

Entitlement vs Experience

"We live in an age of instant knowledge. And there's almost a sense of entitlement to that."

- J.J. Abrams

Millennials! Yes, millennials, those of us who were born between 1980-1994, we get hit with the word *entitlement* often. We're often identified by what many calls the instant gratification or microwave generation. Don't be mad at me, but I admit my fellow millennials...it's true. Sometimes we want everything right now, but we sometimes are not willing to put in the hard work to obtain it. Since you won't admit it, I'll put myself out there. I use to struggle with waiting on everything and almost anything- the pharmacy drive-thru, money to travel comfortably, weight loss, getting married, relocating, changing careers, looking for the right car, and the list goes on. I had that entitlement spirit like why wait!? Umm...maybe because you're not ready for it right now, maybe because this is going to hurt your finances, or maybe because you really don't need it.

When my daughter became a teenager, who is part of Generation-Z, entitlement brought on a new meaning. I mean it shoved me in the face! I couldn't and still don't understand why one feels so entitled to something as though the sun rises and sets on their time. Sad, but this was a lot of us. Having kids would change your whole gratitude attitude about entitlement. It wasn't until then I understood how I missed so many opportunities, because I felt entitled to-I should be, have or doing this and that, because of this or that. All entitlement...

I could recall when I was working for a well-known organization, I planned my own career development in my head about my future with this organization. I anticipated on getting promoted within six months to a year and thought it's no way I shouldn't. I felt entitled for several reasons; I was black and female, so was my supervisor, I'm a person of faith, just like my supervisor, and we had the same degree, while some in the organization didn't have one at all. We had several things in common plus we were surely getting closer than just co-workers, we started to talk more like friends, she shared things with me about upper management that a supervisor wouldn't usually do and she invited me to her family's Christmas party. My millennial self said, *"Oh I got this, of course I'm getting this promotion!"* Well, I was wrong...I didn't get the promotion in the time I expected, so I sought employment elsewhere, and left. Wrong move! Before making such an irrational decision I didn't consider I was undeveloped for certain roles on the job or something else will come around that would better fit my skill set. I had experienced a setback in my career because of my entitlement attitude.

Experiences are just that...experiences. It helps us to grow and learn from our silly mistakes. It gives us something that we cannot adopt in any other way. In order to appreciate and flourish with who you are and what you have to offer, you must be

grateful for those experiences you have been granted. Please Note: Sometimes God uses unexpected encounters to bring unexpected blessings.

Forgiveness vs. Future

"True forgiveness is when you can say, Thank you for the experience."

- Oprah Winfrey

According to the nonprofit Fetzer Institute, 62 percent of American adults say they need more forgiveness in their personal lives (*Fetzer Institute, 2010*). I'm mindful that forgiveness is quite a heavy subject and weight on your shoulders. Forgiving ourselves is less likely to do than forgiving others. How many times have you heard a victim feel bad for staying in an abusive relationship, or a person blaming themselves for getting raped? I didn't know how powerful forgiveness was until I needed forgiveness for myself. Granted, we all have made some horrible, unreasonable, silly decisions that have caused us to be either guilty or shameful about our actions or what happened to us.

Ok, I'm going to let you in on something I never told a soul until now, so you're the first to know. I once slept with a married man. This event in my life tormented me for years. When I met this man I had no knowledge of him being married. He lied to me, he had a whole family and my naive self at the time didn't know to ask certain questions. Questions like, "Are you married? "Are you involved with anyone?", "Do you have children?" or "Are you crazy as hell?" I just thought if this man is talking to me all the time and we're hanging out, of course he's not married.

Ok, I can hear you saying..." Well, you didn't know." You're right, at one point I didn't know. But not so fast! After being upset about it for a couple of weeks and telling him about himself, I slept with him again. Most will call this a homewrecker at least that what I will think of myself every time I left his presence. This crushed me and shamed me for years. My thoughts were here I am sleeping with a married man knowing how I felt being a wife before. I've always respected the covenant of marriage. I asked myself how and why was I at this place. It was another episode of me being disappointed in myself, and also not truly loving myself.

    I'm not sure what you have ever been ashamed of, but one thing I am sure of is that we all have dealt with something that we have or we will have to forgive ourselves for something. I had to face myself in the mirror and accept what I had done. I asked myself some deep-rooted questions; such as why didn't I stop when I knew better. I had to make a decision and stop all communication with him. Again, forgiveness is not easy, rather it's for yourself or to give someone else, but it's necessary. It's necessary for your heart and mental health. I finally forgave myself when I thought about God's grace. In 2 Corinthians 12:9, it states *"My grace is sufficient for you, for your power is made perfect in weakness"*, meaning God has already paid for our sins knowingly we would have some weak moments throughout life's journey. When I finally received this wholeheartedly, I was grateful for God's grace and no longer wanted to disappoint Him in that way. I realized what I did was not who I was nor would it dictate what God has for my future. There is certainly freedom in forgiveness.

GED vs. GYM (Giants Ends Desires vs Guard Your Mind)

"The one way to get me to work my hardest was to doubt me."

-Michelle Obama

Imagine this: here is a person, who is pretty intelligent, made decent grades, never gotten into any real trouble, member of the National Honor Society, and can ball on the court, but never could pass just one test by 1 to 2 points to obtain a high school diploma. If you haven't guessed it by now- this was me. No, I didn't receive my high school diploma-only a high school completion certificate, because of this piece of crappy standardized test Florida called the FCAT. Although, I completed all twelve years of school diligently, I couldn't get what I worked so hard for at the end. Can you imagine how crushed I was? Every year since the 10th grade, I would take this test and miss the math portion by 1 to 2 points. This giant in my life set me back big time! Especially mentally!

Unfortunately, I fell into a deep depression, I no longer knew what I wanted to do anymore or what I wanted to become. I realized I had lost my desire to hurry up and go get my GED. It was no surprise that I was intimidated by another "BIG" test. I was haunted and bound by this unfinished disaster. You can be mentally strong, yet emotionally checked out, and spiritually wounded.

It wasn't until 2009, six years after high school, when I decided to conquer my giant. I admit I didn't pass the GED test the very first time I took it. Yep, it was that damn math portion again. This time I had a new attitude about it though. I adopted a "go getter" attitude. I was also determined to get in the "gym" mentally, focus and knock this giant down! I was determined to guard my mind against my dyslexia disabilities, embarrassment, my anxiety about testing and most of all prove to myself that I can conquer anything. It went back and took it immediately. I'm forever grateful to have gone through the whole test giant experience because it taught me resilience. I haven't been the same since. Today, I read nonstop and study anything and everything that helps me grow mentally. I've had a business where I had to learn math that was understandable to me, received my psychology degree and I'm now in graduate school obtaining my Master's Degree in Nonprofit Business Leadership Management and not to mention hold a few great certifications. So, what are the giants *you* need to face? International motivational speaker, Les Brown once shared advice a woman once told him, "Until you handle something with grace it will stay in your face." You can also be grateful for your giants when you take charge of them.

Habits vs. Health

"Chaos isn't good for your health"

- India Arie

Oftentimes, when people mention health, they generally think of the physical portion only. Although physical health is important, our emotional, spiritual, and mental health is just as essential. While working and living in the downtown area, I would see homeless people walking and talking to themselves in an excessive manner. Some walked with their heads down, slept on the sidewalks, and some carried bottles in their hands. I would even see some with a huge coat on in the middle of a hot summer day in July. I used to always wonder, I mean literally imagined what could have happened in some of those people's lives that would cause them to lose a sense of being. Well, I got a glimpse of how when met Mr. Navy.

One day a co-worker and I had the honor of speaking with a pleasant homeless man, who asked us to call him Mr. Navy. We were doing what we have done plenty of times before, feeding the community. On this particular day, Mr. Navy shared his story with us. He didn't seem as though he was like the other homeless people we would come across. Surprisingly, he was once a former physician in the United States Navy with a wife and three daughters. Unfortunately, he had a huge gambling problem that turned into a horrible drinking problem. One thing I know for sure - bad habits often cause a reduction in cash, corruption, and lousy connections. After his wife left him due to his continuously poor habits and bad decisions it caused him more pain. As a result, his habits got worse. He lost his job, home, friends and connection with his family. He later confessed how he could have reconciled with one of his daughters, but later found out she passed away while he was on the streets. I wish I could say he got off the streets after such loss, but Mr. Navy decided to stay on the streets after this incident. He never explained why in that moment.

    See, when we're young we usually take our health for granted. The toxic foods, drugs, constant alcohol consumption, various sex partners, and any other habits that are not best for us aren't taken into consideration. We let those things enter our bodies, minds and souls and don't consider the long-term effect it has on our overall health. In my 20's, I didn't prioritize my health. I later cultivated that skill. I realized if my mental health is not grounded, nothing else would function properly. Just think our mental health affects our emotions by how we feel and how we control those feelings. It affects our physical by what we consume in our bodies. It also affects our peace spiritually by functioning in dysfunction.

    Mr. Navy later said he could have been back on his feet and living good again, but he likes telling people his story. I thought to myself how could this homeless man, who is so smart continue to speak with such joy, smile and laugh while he's telling his story. It told me one thing- he was still grateful to have his memories. Consider this takeaway: Your habits build character. Be grateful for the body and mind you have been given and take care of it the best you can, because it's our health that gets us through many stages in life. You should never take your health for granted. Even if you're not in the best of health as of today, you can still be grateful for life.

Part 2: JOB/CAREER/BUSINESS

"I WOULD HATE TO DIE AND NEVER DO WHAT I WAS BORN TO DO."

- Bishop T.D. Jakes

Incarceration vs. Information

"Everything is at all times just as it needs to be!"

-Iyanla Vanzant

In 2004, Akon, a music artist released a song called "Locked Up". The lyrics were, *"I'm locked up, they won't let me out, they won't let me out..."* The song became very catchy along with the beat that coordinated very well with it. Well, this song reminded me exactly how I felt when I use to work at this call center job I once had. Locked up! I was incarcerated-trust me! Now you might say that isn't nothing, are you serious, especially if you actually been incarcerated before. Therefore, I apologize in advance, I'm not trying to offend anyone, but this is how I felt working on that particular job.

Many of us have been somewhat locked up on a job in our own minds, and they wouldn't let us out by offering better compensation, competitive benefits to support us, or not giving us the time off when it was needed. I literally went to this job for a little over 10 months and hated every single day I got up to go. If you have never worked in a call center, allow me to explain. I was working with a health insurance company call center, and I was responsible for providing benefit information to doctor's offices regarding their patients. I was so sick of quoting HMO, PPO and whatever coverage. We had to make sure we took care of a certain amount of calls each day and here is the worst part - we were required to notify the manager when we needed to use the restrooms. Might I add, having a poor manager didn't help the work atmosphere either. Locked up...right? Well, when I finally decided to leave this job I was ecstatic! No, I don't think you understand, I can't find the words to express to you how thrilled I was to get off those phones. I wouldn't even get on my personal phone after work, I use to frown when I would see someone calling me after work. Due to this form of incarcerated state I was in, I said to myself during that time I would never go back in anyone's call center. I haven't since.

Although, I didn't like that call center experience, later I realized God has a way of showing you he puts us in a certain place for a reason. This is called an assignment. At that same job I met a great friend, who I'm still friends with today and gained an abundance amount of information. Information and knowledge that still serves me today. We may not always like our occupation experiences or duties, but learn to be grateful for them. You may be at that job to get in contact with someone for your future. Because of the information I inherited, I never looked at another job the same. I thank you, Aetna!

Job vs. Joy

"Don't settle for happiness when you can have joy."

- Anonymous

When I left Aetna, I went to work for a law firm. I said ok, it's time for me to use my paralegal skills which is why I went back to school initially and do something I think I might enjoy. You've probably heard the phrase before that JOB=**J**ust **O**ver **B**roke. Well, at this job this wasn't my story- for the first time I was making some really great money, plus I was getting bonuses, and would sometimes travel to Orlando, Florida for work. It was lit or dope-whatever you want to insert here to know it was the bomb! Hell, I was grateful for the money at the time, happy that I could finally plan a decent future for myself. I was even thinking about going through with law school, yes, I was that excited about the future.

However, this job was extremely stressful. I took work home, had to answer my phone on the weekends while I was hanging out or spending time with my daughter, and I dealt with outrageous clients on a regular basis. My happiness started to decline when I saw I wasn't making it to church on Sundays or able to spend quality time with my family. Why? I know why...because I was so eager to close a case to get more money. Don't get me wrong, there's nothing wrong with having money or wanting money, but I've learned to not allow money or material things to control you. Unfortunately, I had to go through this lesson a few times, but I finally got it. We have to learn that those things that brings us pure joy are not materialistic. Real happiness cannot be purchased. My friend, that law firm went bankrupt and closed down, and as a result, I was unemployed. This was the same job

I mentioned earlier about the house disappointment. I admit I was not by no means happy for losing my job at first, but I am grateful I lost it, because I know I probably wouldn't have never left due to money being my idol at the time. Please note: God will take away anything that you are serving more than Him. Money can be taken away, but joy cannot.

Knight vs. Knowledge

"Knowledge will give you power, but good character will give you respect."

-Dr. Dharius Daniels, Ewing, NJ.

Leadership can be rough. I've seen it, heard stories about it, and experienced it. Ok, let me ask you this - have you ever heard of the phrase "Captain save-a-hoe"? I'm sure you have and yes the Christian said hoe. Hoe is in the bible! Geez! Just in case you don't know let me school you. Captain save-a-hoe is a person who is trying to rescue someone else or multiple of people from something that is usually not their responsibility to do. That simple.

I've been fortunate to have some successful intelligent friends, who are supervisors, brick and mortar business owners, and CEO's. Everyone is a leader in their own right. I could remember when my friend Sheila and I received our degrees together, I majored in Psychology and she majored in Business, then accepted a lucrative career at a prestigious organization right after graduation. Shelia was very knowledgeable about her role as a specialist and took the initiative to climb the corporate ladder. As time went by on the job, she would call me during the week to vent about how she had to "save a hoe" because they didn't know their job. I think what made Sheila angry the most about being a "Captain" in her office is when someone would have a higher position than her and didn't know what they were doing.

For four years, Sheila was trying to land the Lead Director position, but could never obtain it. After a random meeting from their

District Manager asking for a performance test, Sheila was finally promoted. Unfortunately, under Sheila's leadership, she started to get high turnover in her department and lack of respect. Some of the other employees no longer had a "captain save a..." to rescue them from their duties. As a result, the organization suffered from poor performance from the employees, because of the lack of knowledge. Sheila, subsequently stepped down from her position went to another department. She shared with me how much she learned from the experience as a leader.

In that season, we both were grateful to have discovered two components of leadership. As a leader, you cannot do the work for others, but you must inspire and encourage them to carry their own load. Lastly, be grateful for timing. Just because you desire a title that does not mean it's your time.

Longsuffering vs. Longevity

"Struggle is a never ending process. Freedom is never really won, you earn it and win it in every generation."

- Coretta Scott King

    I wish I could just say long suffering produces endurance, which is good for your character, because it then produces hope. But it's not that simple, especially when you are in the midst of the suffering. When I researched the word "longsuffering" I saw words attached to it like mild, gentle, meek, patient, and humble. If you ever waited on something worth having, you have to cross all five of those words associated with threshold. Longsuffering is not fun, but in the process it teaches us to be more gentle with others, patient with the process, (because we have no choice at the time) and to be humble in order to remain grounded. When I used to work on certain jobs, I didn't want the longsuffering part of the journey. Have you ever been on your breaking point at a job or called in often, because you couldn't see the progress of your labor? I understand I've been there along with others I'm sure of it. Then, I think about how those people who fought for civil rights must have felt.

    I visit Atlanta very often, but sometime last year when I was there, I visited the newly renovated Dr. Martin Luther King, Jr. and Coretta Scott King National Historical Park and Museum. It was absolutely breathtaking! I left there thinking *what in the world could I possibly complain about?* As I walked around this grand museum and read several commemorative plaques, I started to get teary-eyed, because I could only imagine how much forbearing Dr. Martin Luther King, Jr. and his noble wife had to go through during the civil rights movement. They were constantly beaten and threatened throughout his work, yet he endured. Therefore, due to Dr. King's obedience and longsuffering we now get to reap from his unwavering efforts. He was so unmovable and dedicated to his work with the end goal in mind- he couldn't and didn't waiver.

    Regardless of where you are, I advise you to not give up, but to be grateful for whatever work you are assigned to do in this season. It is the longsuffering that makes you appreciate the longevity. I believe gratitude eases the pain when longsuffering becomes too heavy of a burden to bear.

Not yet vs. Now

"When times get though we don't give up. We get up."

-President Barack Obama

While I was working in family and criminal law, I can remember coming in contact with various cases. I would hear some horror stories of people's day-to-day lives. I'm talking murder, battery, domestic violence, sexual assault, child support, and of course nasty divorce cases. These cases gave me a lot of insight on how rapidly a person would move to get out of their present situation. My attorney supervisor, Linn, at the time taught me three things that always influenced me when working with anyone, especially business clients. The three things are value, urgency, and rapport. He would say "find out what's the value of the call, meaning what service do they need. How urgent do they need the service, meaning how important is it to them right now. Finally, build a rapport by the information you now know." I absolutely love Linn's strategies and still use it when conducting business today.

People would call in a demanding matter wanting to get things handled, so they can benefit from some kind of concord in their lives. They needed to move forward NOW! Sometimes when we're faced with hardships it pushes us to make a NOW move instead of a not yet. My NOW is the very reason you are holding this book. I said not yet to numerous of things over and over. For instance, I put writing a book off for years. I would start and stop and say those words "not yet". Why not yet? Money. Time. Those were my excuses. It wasn't until an urgency appeared that a change in my circumstances reversed my attitude from not yet to NOW. I knew someone needed this book. You may have to sacrifice time and money, but once you get activated in your NOW you won't regret it.

Question: What if Jesus would have said not yet? What if King Tuck would have said not yet, Beyonce, or Oprah? When you're grateful for your gifts and talents you wouldn't say not yet, but you'll say I have to NOW. Also, when you're hopeful about what your future will bring you even when things don't look so great at the moment, you'll start NOW.

Oppression vs. Opportunity

"I freed a thousand slaves, I could have freed a thousand more if only they knew they were slaves"

- Harriet Tubman

I could remember back in grade school when we were taught about American history, Greek history, some Asian history, yet not much about Black history. Of course, we had little discussions about Dr. Martin Luther King Jr., Carter G. Woodson, Madam CJ. Walker and a few other nobles. The great leader Nelson Mandela, was never mentioned to me until I read about him on my own has an adult. I say very often one who does not read nor study will remain a "slave". I'm not talking about doing a Google search on everything either! I'm referring to actually studying from written hardcopy books, articles, and journals. Nelson Mandela was one of the reasons I became inspired to want to attend law school. As previously mentioned, it never worked out for me. I resigned from my law school dream for a number of reasons. Go back to the "M's" if you missed it. Later, I read how Mandela obtained his law degree while jailed in Pretoria, South Africa prison. While going through a great deal of oppression he still sought out opportunity to gather education, so he could better represent an ideal democratic and free society in which others could live in harmony.

I can relate to the late Nelson Mandela to an extent, I've had to overcome hideous predicaments that caused sleepless nights, depression, but overcoming gave me the opportunity to do what I love to do today…help free others from mental despair. When things are not so great, because of your oppression-find your opportunity to serve with gratitude, and you'll be pleased you did. Please note: It's in our oppression when we find our opportunities.

Part 3: RELATIONSHIPS

"YOU'RE BORN LOOKING LIKE YOUR PARENTS, BUT YOU DIE LOOKING LIKE YOUR DECISIONS."

-Pastor Keion Henderson

Processing Parenting

"Fall in love with the process, and the results will come."

- Eric Thomas

Just a couple of months before my 21st birthday, at age 20 years old I became a mother to a beautiful, hairy nine pound, twenty-one inches' baby girl at 5:05pm on a warm Thursday afternoon. My late ex-husband and I had only been married eleven months. Talk about having to grow up fast! I remember us going out buying all kinds of unnecessary things, such as a suburban SUV. Our families would make comments like "Geez, how many kids y'all having?" We discussed having two kids, but we only had one. My Kayla.

My parents are baby-boomers, so growing up we had little to no opinion at all regarding what we wanted. What they said went and that was it. Period! End of story. Done. I carried some of those same concepts in my parenting style to an extent. Remember earlier I mentioned how this new generation, those who are born in the 2000's and up has this sense of entitlement on another level? Well, they do! They somewhat feel entitled that they should have some kind of explanation - why they can't have or do something. I came to the realization that saying "Because I said so" doesn't always work. Although, I still sometimes say those disheartening words to my now teenager, I became aware as time progressed that I had to change my parenting style to whatever stage my daughter is in. For example, when Kayla was in middle school, she must have gone to demon nation and came back. I'm kidding, but those years were very challenging for us both. I would punish her, but not discipline her. I would yell, take away things she enjoyed, and ground her for weeks. I wouldn't listen to her reasoning why she would act the way she did. All I knew was the behavior wasn't acceptable in my sight.

      Later, I realized I was doing to her what was being done to me while growing up. She was not that little kid anymore that didn't know how to properly express her viewpoint. I was failing as a parent and not processing parenting as well as I thought I was. My home wasn't prospering the way I imagined it to. The older people would say it wasn't in order. As parents, we can't just punish them and not give them wisdom. Don't be mistaken here - I still have to set the law and say, "Kayla, that's it, I've made my decision." Of course, children don't understand that you're trying to protect them from any destructive decisions. When we were teenagers we didn't understand either, remember? No, we as parents are not given a step-by-step manual for parenting. Look, when it comes to parenting, no matter how many books you read to prepare for different stages- it doesn't compare to actually experiencing it. I have become grateful for the parenting process. Even in the not so great days, weeks, and sometimes a few months, I am grateful God has blessed me with the responsibility to raise another human being. I'm also grateful for my parents for instilling a great amount of tact in me. As you get older, you realize your

parents have stories too and do the best they can with what they have. Nevertheless, Kayla has taught me the true meaning of leadership, teamwork, patience, and unconditional love, and for these things I'm grateful indeed.

Quality vs. Quantity

"Associate yourself with people of good quality, for it is better to be alone than in bad company."

–Booker T. Washington

    Growing up I never had many friends by choice. I have always been quiet until I entered high school, and even then only associated with a few. Today, I'm still that observant and reserved individual. Once we both get to know each other more, you would find me more talkative. I call myself an outgoing introvert. I have always been amazed how some would seem to have thousands of friends. Don't get me wrong- it's certainly nothing wrong with having a lot of friends, if that's your prerogative. Some people get a serious high from being around others. Not me! I mainly associate my time with people who will add value to me, and vice versa. To be honest, I haven't always been the greatest friend - I took some really great friendships for granted and neglected the quality that we once shared. How did this happen, you wonder? Well, let's just say I got out of my true character trying to gain validation for some to either notice my qualities, immaturity took place or simply just being a people pleaser.

    After doing much self-reflection, I learned the true value of having great people in my life to enhance me. It's nothing wrong with few- God has always done a lot with few. A few loaves of bread feed thousands, a few oil drops anointed a King. I'm grateful for my genuine few. Consider this: Find people who would add to your growth, inspire you, challenge you to be better and don't waste your time on things that are not important. Be grateful for those people that come into your life and do these things. Quality trumps quantity every day!

Rejection vs. Reflection

"What feels like punishment is preparation and protection."

-Anonymous

Ok, let me just say this I for one love "RE" words; such as regroup, reform, refocus, regarding, refer, retrieve, reflect, and even rejection. Yep! The big yucky word...rejection.

Rejection is something that is sneaky. It's looked upon as a negative perception. Sometime or another we all have dealt with rejection, as early as pre-school, a kid has a toy you wanted to play with - he takes it and gives it to someone else. In grade school, all the cool kids sit at the same lunch table together and never invite you to sit with them, maybe it was the girl who rejected your prom proposal to go with someone else (by the way I did this to someone.), or perhaps your job dismissed your idea and went with another idea instead. These are all forms of rejection, and while I probably did not mention your specific rejection, we all have experienced some sort of rejection in our lifetime.

I've always had a struggle with rejection until I became aware of who I am. Every now and then, I still have to give myself a self-talk and reiterate, "Well it must be a reason why this or that didn't happen the way I wanted it to." In addition, I had to come to terms with why I'm the daughter that got molested (not that I wish it would have happened to someone else), why I'm the girl boys never really asked out in high school to date, why I never got recognition for my basketball skills, why my marriage didn't work out, or why I never got the promotions at work. As we grow, we have the tendency to look back at our past and reflect. Reflection is a good way to gain gratitude even when your experiences weren't so great.

    All those things were substance for who I am today. If I never would have gotten abused, I probably wouldn't know how to be compassionate towards others. If I would have gotten recognized for my basketball skills, I probably wouldn't be as humble as I am today, and if my marriage would have worked I probably wouldn't know how to fully forgive. My friend, God has a way of using one thing and making it a blessing to set you up for your future. Reflect on your rejections and be grateful some things didn't work out or go through as planned.

Separation vs. Strength

"What you focus on the longest-you become the strongest."

-Les Brown

On September 4, 2004, I married my high school sweetheart, Christopher A. Maiten. Everything happened so fast, so keep up! Chris was a very polite, sweet, athletic, giving young man, with a great sense of humor and stubborn as a bull. Before we had gotten married, Chris decided to go into the United States Army Reserves. Shortly, after we got married, he decided to go full-time in the army that October. Sad to say, but that November we found out Chris would be deployed to Iraq for twelve months in December. Here we are newly-weds and just received the news we were not expecting -at least not that soon. My heart was young and heavy. I didn't know what was to come of this type of transition. December came and we found out we were expecting. I was pregnant and alone while Chris went off to deployment after the holidays.

This separation tossed me into a deep depression, and being pregnant didn't help my moods either. I wouldn't go anywhere, I no longer worked in that season and remind you I still had that high school FCAT test lingering in my face during this time. All I would do is eat, vomit, sleep, and attend my doctor's appointments. Sad, I know. I talked so negative to myself, my mind wouldn't let me focus on anything else, but my depressing condition. Why wasn't I grateful that I was married to the love of my life, being provided for with no complaints, or ecstatic about carrying a blessing in my stomach? I was horrible at this test in life. Please note: Sometimes God will send you the same test in a different formula to help you grow through what you need to learn. After eight years of Chris and I knowing each other, life happened and we grew apart. We were young and both had our own personal struggles as young people at the time we did not resolve or was aware how to. In the hot summer of August in 2011, I went through the same test of separation. This time it was because of the wretched word-divorce! We didn't go through a nasty divorce like some do, but it was still hard. I had bouts of depression here and there, but that's normal. Going through a divorce is a grieving process. I was losing something that was a part of me I'd known eight years of my life. Although I was losing my marriage, lost my job, and had to move back to my mom's house, I remained hopeful for the future. I went back to school, enrolled in college, worked two jobs and focused on our daughter. I was in a different element in this season. I adopted strength. I wish I could end this separation fever right here, but this wasn't it...Life took its course once again.

      Chris and I got separated one last time. On November 9, 2012, three days after my birthday, I received a call from my sister-n-law asking where was I and telling me to get somewhere settled, my spirit knew before she could even get the first syllabus out. Something was terribly wrong. The words rolled out her mouth into my cynical ears. Chris had committed suicide. Of course, I never experienced such disturbing news until now. My stomach dropped. I use to look at suicide as a selfish act, but going through this incident I became more compassionate and self-aware of mental illness. Clearly this is what Chris suffered from. You see; Chris was deployed three different times to Iraq and Afghanistan while he was in the Army, and severely suffered from PTSD and schizophrenia from his journeys. I'll say he just couldn't mentally bare anymore hurt. Chris was my great friend even after our divorce and loving provider to our daughter. I thought I had strength before, but I never knew how much strength I had until my final separation with him. I'm thankful I am a part of his legacy and I will always honor him. Find a way to be grateful for those who have enhanced your life in any way.

Traditions vs. Teachings

"Traditions becomes our security, and when the mind is secure it is in decay."

-Jidda Krishnamurti

Traditions have a way of controlling us, yet shaping who we will become. All cultures have some sort of commemoration of occasion; such as weddings, sororities/fraternities, birthdays, holiday gatherings, school preferences, food selections, career decisions, and religion all has its own custom or tradition. Some traditions I followed, and some I did not. As you have read earlier, you can see I definitely didn't follow a lot of society's traditions. For instance, I did not attend college right after high school (I couldn't), I did not wait to get married, nor do I go to family houses every Christmas, or stay on the same job for twenty plus years because it's "stable" and have good benefits. Nope! However, I was on a strict religion tradition. Geez, I said that like an uneasy diet. In all honesty, I'm grateful for my spiritual background, but there was a time - well let's go there. Ok, so I grew up in a Baptist church. Therefore, a lot of traditions were to be followed. Deaconess wore white on first Sundays for communion, no wearing shorts whatsoever to church, choir robes were pressed - stuff like that. Today, church is a little more relaxed, probably a little too relaxed for some. I could remember waking up to go to church on Sunday mornings for 7:30am service, then head to Sunday school (which I disliked, because they would always try to make me talk), next ate a hot breakfast of grits, eggs, bacon, and toast in the church cafeteria. Afterwards, go to 10:45am regular service, either that was in children's church or sitting with friends in the balcony, where we would get fussed at for passing notes and talking. Then, end the Sunday by going back to church in the evening at 5:30pm for night service. We would also attend bible study on Wednesdays and let me dare not fail to mention some Saturdays when we would have choir rehearsal or some sort of outreach event we were involved in. I know that was a lot, but imagine living it. Yep, the Baptist church was a large part of my life growing up. Most of my friends as a child and teenager came from church instead of school, and there are still a few of us who still keep in touch today.

When I grew up, I didn't attend church regularly. I got married and moved away to another state. I couldn't find a church I liked - this was my excuse. I didn't step foot in a weekly bible study session since I was eighteen-years-old until a few years ago. Church people would call this back sliding. Well, I was calling this "freedom" at one point, somewhat like a college student leaving home to attend school out-of-state. You ever notice how some people start to develop a sense of "own" self when they leave their families traditions? This was me regarding the church. I could remember my grandmother and mom asking me on different occasions if I've been to church. I would say no, but felt horrible. I think I felt horrible because I knew who lived inside of me, where my help came from and did not give God his time. But no matter what, I no longer wanted tradition, I yearned for teaching!

One reason I stopped going is because I realized I was going to church out of habit. When I would go sometimes and not really apply what I learned, I stopped going again for three years or so, as mentioned in the introduction of this book. After going through much hell - I was a revelation of what exactly Proverbs 22:6 says, "Train up a child in the way he should go; even when he is old he will not depart from it." Still to this day I'm amazed how I know certain scriptures and old hymns- it was because of my relationship with the church, my upbringing and those teachings my grandmother and mom embedded in me.

Today, I'm a member of a non-denominational church which I have developed great spiritual maturity. I now have a true relationship with God and not just following a religion tradition. I learned to be grateful for those long days in church my mom making me go to Shiloh Metropolitan Baptist Church every Sunday, and it's because of those days from week after week I can share the gospel with others and I have a foundation in God.

Part 4: FAITH

"TRUST IN THE LORD WITH ALL YOUR HEART AND LEAN NOT ON YOUR OWN UNDERSTANDING, IN ALL YOUR WAYS SUBMIT TO HIM, AND HE WILL DIRECT YOUR PATH."

-PROVERBS 3:5-6

Understanding Upgrades

"Don't upgrade your technology more than you upgrade yourself"

- Anonymous

In the beginning of this book I touched on self- awareness. Well, understanding and self-awareness are parallel to one another. For instance, you have to have a better understanding of who you are and know why you are who you are through self- awareness. I was going to save this for the conclusion, but I'll give you a glance here, because I believe your gratitude is starting to activate. Here is my simple formula, actually Bishop T.D. Jakes said it best:

- Relentless- Get you there.

- Consistent- Keep you there.

- Grateful- Will get you more there. I have lived and been tested by this formula and it works, so I thank you Bishop T.D. Jakes for that.

My friend, I want you to understand that you have to upgrade your thinking for your future. How you speak to yourself has power. Remember, you are the first person to hear what you are saying. When I became desperate for God, I didn't care what sacrifice it took, I just knew I needed to be in His will for my life. I had to upgrade my faith, believe that God can and will work things out for me. Second, I had to incorporate consistency in my life. For years, I went back and forth with upgrading my life and walk with God, but when I developed consistency, my faith and understanding strengthened. Lastly, as mentioned throughout this book I had to be grateful where I was in life to fully appreciate who God was.

- I had to understand greatness made me, so greatness is in me.

- I had to understand my mistakes and past does not determine who I am, but it's what I did.

- Understand you have to be willing to let people go without giving notice in your upgrading process.

- Understand your most unexpected blessings comes from being grateful.

Proverbs 4:7

Victim vs. Vision

"A man without a vision for his future will always return to his past"

- Marcus Garvey

When one has been a victim of any kind, it's hard to see a clear future for yourself. I've learned that healing takes time and it's not smart to put your deadline on anyone else's deliverance. With me being a victorious victim of molestation, from ages 9 to nearly 17 years old off and on I experienced this first hand. Victimization can demolish your whole outlook on life if you let it. I used to wonder if this or that hadn't happened to me what I would have become. Truth is, that's irrelevant. I apologize for being somewhat casual about what I'm saying, but it's true. It's irrelevant to think or care about what you would have been. I am who I am today, because of such an unfortunate circumstance.

People who I have shared my story with ask me how I got over something so detrimental. My answer is it's not that I necessarily got over it - God delivered me and I had to make a decision to forgive. You never get over something that victimizes you; however, you go through the process of healing. I asked God to give me a vision for my life. I no longer wanted to be angry, passive-aggressive, and paranoid. If I never went through my healing, I would have never found the purpose for my life. I wouldn't have never taken an interest in psychology, advocacy, pursuing a nonprofit organization for girls, or doing what I do for a living now as a Certified Victims Advocate. Your victimization may not be in comparison to my story. For some, it might be divorce, procrastination, fear, or selfishness. I hope whatever it is keeping you bound, you find the courage and strength to release it.

I'm grateful that God used my messy twisted story for His glory to help heal others, encourage, and give someone hope. My healing process might be different from yours, but if you don't get anything out of this passage, Please Note: God sees you and cares for you. Get pass your past, so you can press forward on your future.

Psalms 33:20

Want vs Wisdom

"Don't buy your wants and beg for your needs"

- John C. Maxwell

      I once heard a preacher say "instructions come before structure." Now let me tell you my hard headed butt didn't understand this until I kept making detours in life. While writing this part of my book, I can't stop grinning, because I just think about all the stupid things I used to do just because I didn't wait on my wants. I mentioned earlier how I felt entitled to my wants. To be honest, I know I probably would be further along in life if I would have just waited on some things I wanted instantly. However, I am beyond grateful for my lessons. Let me tell you, I had a pattern of wanting a certain job, car, house, friends - you name it and they were not in God's will for me at the time. After losing enough money and struggling, I realized I was getting older and I couldn't afford to make the same mistakes. I simply asked for wisdom, because God knows I need it. Here was one of my prayers: Lord, if it doesn't come from you or it's not the right time don't let me get distracted, better yet don't even let it present itself please. I was talking about everything you hear me! - A job, home, friends, a man, and even a church.

      Of course, God had to put my faith to the test. I have peeped him out-this is how God tests us to see if we're going to be obedient. Well, another "want" presented itself. I wanted to relocate to another state. I prayed about it and God sent me a vision where I would be, so you can only imagine how overjoyed I was. I saved my money, start looking for a job, asked others to pray for me, and actually start visiting the city my soul desired. Every time I would go there, I felt a sense of peace over me. I was just so happy that I finally prayed about something and obeyed God's instruction. Well, not so fast! It was 3am and for some reason God always wake me up during that hour to show me something. My spirit told me he's not going to move me until 1-2 years, instead of sooner. You know what I did? I tried to go back to sleep. I wasn't trying to hear that. I really didn't want to accept that. I went back and forth with my thoughts and feelings. My emotions would usually stir my decision that I would later on regret. Suddenly, I thought about the story of David. After David was anointed by God, he sent him right back to the field to work, he didn't send him to his palace right away to be king. Although, God showed David his promise he didn't give him the position yet. I believe sometimes God does this to us so that we can finish out whatever assignment he has placed us in at that time to gather more endurance or knowledge for what's to come. God's desires for our lives are always better than ours.

Today, I'm grateful I finally listened to God and leaned on his wisdom for the plans for my future. Waiting is not always easy, but's necessary when it's instructed.

Psalms 32:8

X-ray Your Heart

"It's hard to be hateful when you're grateful."

- Chris Hogan

The quote I chose for this passage speaks for itself. Yes, it's hard to be hateful when you're grateful. The tenth commandment says "Thou shall not covet", I didn't clearly understand this until I realized that while the other commandments result in behaviors, covet result in one's thoughts. Let me explain. Most of the time those thoughts lead to other behavior that are commandments we shall not do; such as murder, steal, or commit adultery. I happen to love David's story in the bible, so I reference a lot of lessons out of it. Let me give you a brief background.

King David started to lust for one of his soldier's wife, who was named Bathsheba. He saw her bathing one day and was head over hills from there. He asked around who she was and even after it was confirmed she was someone else's wife, he could care less. David got caught up big time, because he coveted something that belonged to another man. While the soldier was away on duty, David finally took his chance to sleep with Bathsheba. Not only did he sleep with his soldier's wife, but here's the real juice - she became pregnant! David was jacked up by that news and did not want to be discovered for his sin. David went so far as to tell the soldier to come home from duty to sleep with his wife to cover up with what has taken place. Unfortunately, the soldier would not sleep with Bathsheba due to his level of focus for his mission.

Here's the sad part - David ordered for him to be on the frontline of war, so he could be killed and he was brutally assassinated!

Sad story, but true. How many of these same stories occur in today's world? How often have you heard about individuals being jealous of something or what someone else has and is willing to take it by any means necessary. My friend, I challenge you to x-ray your heart. When you are grateful for whatever God has provided for you, it is hard to be lustful, envious, and hateful. By being grateful for others, God also sends you blessings. Try to be happy for others even when things are not so great for you, because seasons do change. One thing of many I have learned about God is that He will provide you with the desires of your heart, if it's in His will. I have a saying that I live by: Only a fool envies someone who does something better or have something more than them. Don't be jealous, learn from them!

Psalm 51:10

Youth vs. Youthfulness

"Young lions lack food and go hungry, but those who seek the Lord will not lack no good thing."

-Psalms 34:10

When we're young we often don't stop to think we really don't know a whole lot. We go through our teens and early twenties thinking we have so much time to make things happen, but think we know more than we really do. I could remember being on a family trip in New York City with my mom, sister and my aunts. I was around 18 or 19 years old, and my mom and I got into some type of heavy discussion that I apparently didn't agree with. Well, I murmured under my breath something I can't even remember before saying these words - "*She thinks she knows everything.*" My sonic ear big sister heard me and got me all the way together. Now if my mom would have heard me, who knows what would have happened. Luckily I'm still here to tell the story. I'm glad it was my sister who straightened me out, and not my mom. Sweet lady she is, but she will snatch you up really quick! I'm 35 and I'm still a believer.

After my sister told me how disrespectful I was being, she said something that who knew I would someday say to my own daughter. She said "she's 25 years older than you, why wouldn't she know more...". I have never forgotten that or how it made me feel. It makes sense. Why wouldn't someone have more wisdom, who's being around longer than us? Silly to not think this way, but when you're young you do. I was young, lacked wisdom and "food" the Psalmist from my quote above was talking about. Being young-minded will leave you "hungry", if you don't ask for wisdom or listen to it when it's given.

Please Note: There is a difference between young and youthfulness. For example, in 1 Corinthians 13:11 reads "When I was a child, I spoke as a child, but when I became a man, I put away childish things." However, in Matthew 18:3 reads "Truly, I say to you, unless you turn and become like children, you will never enter the kingdom of heaven." These passages are saying this: When we are children, yes we say and do silly things, because our minds are not yet elevated to think of consequences or have the fear of them, but as we get older (grown) we must become wiser and manage our life decisions. Sometimes this doesn't feel so great. Let's be real, sometimes we all get tired of adult-ing, but at the same time, we dare not go back to someone telling us what to do. Furthermore, God wants us to go to Him like children, full of joy and teachable. Just like children usually don't care about what ethnicity or gender they play with at the playground, they're just joyous to be playing, they also need discipline from authority to learn rules and a form of structure, yet they are still trusting and full of hope. I have a blog on my website titled, "Enjoy your Youth." Be grateful for your youthfulness by enjoying each day simply because you're still amongst the living. When things are not so great, you can still be grateful while adult-ing. As adults, we can enjoy life like children, by having fun, laughing, being open to instruction, and most importantly being full of hope. I learned that God cares about our successes and future as we do our own children.

Psalms 71:17

Zealous Servant

"Do not despise these small beginnings, for the Lord rejoices to see the work begin..."

- Zechariah 4:10

By now your gratitude should have shifted your attitude. If not, my apologies, but I have one more passage for you. In 5th grade, at Susie Tolbert Elementary School, my teacher Ms. Peoples was the absolute best teacher I ever encountered. She had pretty long hair and a lazy eye, but could still see everything that went on in class like none other. I still don't know how that was possible. She was also the teacher that punished me the most. After getting through the kinks of our teacher-student relationship, Ms. Peoples would have me help her with several tasks, she even let me go over to her house after school sometimes. I'm not sure how my mom and her got so acquainted enough for me to explore her home, but I can remember going over there on some occasions Ms. Peoples' home looked like it belonged to a teacher, I recall her having blue curtains and some kind of apple decor all over the house. She's one of the reasons I love stationery items today, and hope to someday have my own stationary line called *L.S. Maiten*. Who knows?

I could remember being asked by her teenage daughter at the time, what I would like to be when I grow up. Of course, that has always been the #1 famous question for all kids, right?

Anyway, I didn't know what to say, so I think I said something quick. A doctor. I probably said that because I always heard my sister tell people that's what she wanted to be. And today, my sister is a doctor. Spontaneously, Ms. Peoples came back and responded with a big smile and a word I never heard of, she said, "but she's a zealous worker." Zealous? I didn't know Ms. Peoples were saying I'm dedicated, diligent or passionate until I heard this again 20 years later from my supervisor, who bought me a bracelet with the words passionate engraved on it. I've always been passionate since the beginning. Think: what's your beginning?

    Ok I'm sure you're asking what's the point. My point is being grateful for your small beginnings; rather you're a student, business owner, spouse or parent shows appreciation for the position. Beginnings are exciting, yet hardly ever the greatest part of the journey. It's a lot of kinks and lessons to be learned. Become a zealous servant, someone who has an absolute unshakable dedication to whatever task you're assigned to. If you have fallen off, it's ok. Get back on and get your gratitude together. I believe God rejoices in our small beginnings, because He knows the gratitude that's in it for us. Be grateful.

Jeremiah 29:11

Ok, one more thing...turn the page.

Epilogue

Romans 8:28 reads *"And we know that for those who love God all things work together for good, for those who are called according to his purpose."* This scripture changed me! My mind shifted in all areas of my life, because of it. It's funny how the first part of the scripture says "And we know"-as though we already have comprehension of something...right? Well, this means to me when you have a relationship with God you know he loves you and you love Him, and this is because you know Him and understand that ALL things - even things that cause us pain, hurt and sorrow still work together for our good, because He is going to use those things for His purpose for us. Why? Because he loves us!

It's really only one way to be grateful when things are not so great--that's changing your mindset. Yes, your thinking! For the most part I've always been an inquisitive individual. I'm naturally curious on how and why things the way they are. This is somewhat tricky though, meaning this can be a good and bad thing. It's a good thing, because it allows you to grow, get an understanding, and gain knowledge. This is true for the bad side too, but the "bad side" process is not so pleasant, but you adopt patience in the midst. Unfortunately, we won't always know how and why things the way they are around us, but I do know Romans 8:28 changed my perspective and attitude about any circumstance I now face.

I don't wish anything foul or horrendous on anyone, including myself. Again, if I would have never been abused, I wouldn't have found my divine purpose. If I never went through an illness, I wouldn't appreciate my health as much as I do now, and it wasn't until

I lost my ex-husband and dear friend to suicide that I sincerely started to value relationships. All things were working together, my friend. In the beginning of this conclusion, I mention that my mind shifted. My mind shifted with my decisions, values, self-worth, and I established great discipline. What does this mean?

Consider this: Seek God first and after you have faith, everything else is added. For example, when I grew in my faith and became grateful for who God was to me, I wanted to love and serve more. First, love and serve God and myself. Truly love and care for who I am as a person. This means I had to establish some values, be mindful of my health - physically and mentally, and think about how I want my future to look financially and regarding relationships. Then, I decided to love and serve others. I no longer did business just to do business, but I wanted to build relationships and serve others with my gifts and talents. All things were working together, my friend. My self-development, my career and business goals, relationships, and my faith. These are the things that are important to me.

No, I'm not near where I would love to be in life or business, but I'm grateful for where I am today. I now have wisdom to endure what life has to offer. Therefore, I'm blessed

beyond measure. I now hope you have unlocked the tools to become grateful when things are not so great!

References

C: Miami Herald. (2010, July 9) *Miami Heat Watch Party [Video file]. Retrieved from https://www.youtube.com/miamiheatwatchparty*

F: Fetzer Institute. (2010) *Fetzer Survey on Love and Forgiveness in American Society*. Pp. 1-6 Available from http://www.fetzer.org

Meet the Author

L.S. Maiten also known as LaRhonda Maiten, is a proud psychology graduate and now non-profit business leadership management student.

As a certified professional and blogger, she enjoys encouraging and educating others to live healthier lives. She resides in Jacksonville, Florida with her daughter.

Learn more and download helpful resources at www.lsmaiten.com

www.ingramcontent.com/pod-product-compliance
Lightning Source LLC
Chambersburg PA
CBHW051705090426
42736CB00013B/2549